A NOTE TO PARENTS

Reading Aloud with Your Child
Research shows that reading books aloud is the single most valuable support parents can provide in helping children learn to read.
- Be a ham! The more enthusiasm you display, the more your child will enjoy the book.
- Run your finger underneath the words as you read to signal that the print carries the story.
- Leave time for examining the illustrations more closely; encourage your child to find things in the pictures.
- Invite your youngster to join in whenever there's a repeated phrase in the text.
- Link up events in the book with similar events in your child's life.
- If your child asks a question, stop and answer it. The book can be a means to learning more about your child's thoughts.

Listening to Your Child Read Aloud
The support of your attention and praise is absolutely crucial to your child's continuing efforts to learn to read.
- If your child is learning to read and asks for a word, give it immediately so that the meaning of the story is not interrupted. DO NOT ask your child to sound out the word.
- On the other hand, if your child initiates the act of sounding out, don't intervene.
- If your child is reading along and makes what is called a miscue, listen for the sense of the miscue. If the word "road" is substituted for the word "street," for instance, no meaning is lost. Don't stop the reading for a correction.
- If the miscue makes no sense (for example, "horse" for "house"), ask your child to reread the sentence because you're not sure you understand what's just been read.
- Above all else, enjoy your child's growing command of print and make sure you give lots of praise. *You are your child's first teacher — and the most important one. Praise from you is critical for further risk-taking and learning.*

— Priscilla Lynch
Ph.D., New York University
Educational Consultant

*For Bev Rogers,
and our New England classroom
—L.B.*

*For two special friends,
Jonathan and Amy Primrose
—S.B.*

*Louise Borden, Steve Björkman, and the editors
would like to thank Jim Baker
of Plimoth Plantation for his expertise.*

Text copyright © 1997 by Louise Borden.
Illustrations copyright © 1997 by Steve Björkman.
All rights reserved. Published by Scholastic Inc.
HELLO READER! and CARTWHEEL BOOKS and associated logos are trademarks and/or registered trademarks of Scholastic Inc.

Library of Congress Cataloging-in-Publication Data

Borden, Louise.
    Thanksgiving is ... / by Louise Borden ; illustrated by Steve Björkman.
       p.   cm.—(Hello reader! Level 3)
    "Cartwheel books."
    Summary: Simply describes how the first Thanksgiving came to be celebrated by the Pilgrims, with a brief mention of some of the traditions that are connected to the holiday today.
    ISBN 0-590-33128-0
    1. Thanksgiving Day—Juvenile literature. 2. United States—Social life and customs—Juvenile literature. [1. Thanksgiving Day 2. Pilgrims (New Plymouth Colony) 3. Massachusetts—History—New Plymouth, 1620-1691.] I. Björkman, Steve, ill. II. Title. III. Series.
GT4975.B67   1997
394.2649—dc21   97-8767
                                             CIP
                                             AC

10 9 8 7 6   9/9 0/0 01 02

Printed in the U.S.A.   24
First printing, October 1997

Thanksgiving Is...

by Louise Borden
Illustrated by Steve Björkman

Hello Reader! — Level 3

SCHOLASTIC INC.

New York   Toronto   London   Auckland   Sydney

It is the fourth Thursday in November, and so it is Thanksgiving.

Thanksgiving is . . .
a long word to spell:

Thanksgiving

longer than

Pilgrim,

or

Mayflower,

or even

New England.

Thanksgiving is . . .
many travelers on a small ship.

Some are Pilgrims.
Some are not.
70 men and women,
32 children,
2 dogs,
no cats,
and a few hens...

all on the Mayflower, together.
The year is 1620.

Thanksgiving is . . .
tall hats with brims,
and ties on shoes,
cloaks in the wind,
and long aprons, too.

Thanksgiving is . . .
stiff, wide collars,
some white on gray.

And Thanksgiving is . . .
a land left behind so Pilgrims
can worship the Pilgrim way.

Thanksgiving is . . .
a long, long trip.
Some travelers are cold.
Some are wet.
Some are sick.

And Thanksgiving is . . .
land at last.
A new land.
New England.

Thanksgiving is . . .
a hard winter in a cold land.
It is a lot of work for all!

Pilgrim fathers cut down trees.
Pilgrim brothers gather thatch.
Pilgrim sisters help Pilgrim mothers.
And all pray for help from God.

Thanksgiving is . . .
men with muskets, off to hunt.
BANG!
BANG! BANG!
Guns glint in the sun.
Fresh meat at last.

Thanksgiving is . . .
Samoset and Squanto,
the Pilgrims' first friends.

Thanksgiving is . . .
corn seed in hills
and nets in the sun.

Thanksgiving is . . .
many hands:

Pilgrim hands,

and Indian hands,

and big hands,
and small hands.

And Thanksgiving is . . .
many hands together.

Thanksgiving is . . .
a Pilgrim harvest in the fall.
And the harvest is good!
Baskets of corn,
baskets of nuts,
bushels of beans and squash.

Fish salted for winter,
then placed in casks.
Wild fowl
and ducks on spits.

Thanksgiving is . . .
a feast for three days,
after the harvest.

And Thanksgiving is . . .
Pilgrims and Indians
together.

Thanksgiving is . . .
gifts without ribbons,
more than 300 Novembers ago.

Thanksgiving is . . .
land and harvest.

Thanksgiving today is from
Thanksgiving back then.

It is grandmas and grandpas,
uncles and aunts!
It is turkey with gravy
and pumpkin pie.
It is football,
and friends,
and big parades!
It is a day to say thanks for blessings,
all over our land.

It is the fourth Thursday in November, and so it is Thanksgiving.